Fellini's Kitchen presents...

KISSING IN THE KITCHEN

The Romantic Comedy Cookbook for Couples

By Stacey Y. Moore

Recipes for lifelong relationships based on movies like: The Five Year Engagement, Date Night, Guess Who and many more…

Copyright © 2014 Stacey Y. Moore
All rights reserved
ISBN-13: 978-1505728019
ISBN-10: 1505728010

Foreword

The bad news...

If you are a newlywed or soon-to-be wed, chances are you have already heard the staggering divorce rate statistics being doled as a cautionary tale by... well, everyone. There are very few media outlets, experts or studies that will tell you that your new marriage is safe. In fact they will tell you that the odds are against you. Not really the type of stuff you wanna hear when you're in the throes of planning the best day of your life, or just after you've spent a ton of cash on the best wedding day you could afford, right?

The good news...

I am not big on shock. I prefer empowerment as a choice. With that said, I am here to tell you and your new spouse:

- You do have the power to avoid becoming another statistic.
- You have the power to enjoy a strong marriage, and you have the power to create a lifelong relationship. Say it with me, "Stronger, longer!"
- What happens to your marriage is up to you and your spouse, not the numbers.

There are tried and true ways for you to invest in the emotional capital of your marriage. I am talking, easy-breezy ways for couples just like you to ensure that your marriage grows stronger and last longer than those couples who choose to leave it all to fait (I call them lazy, I also call them boring). I know what you're thinking. You're thinking that I am gonna say, "it takes hard work." Wrong! It's not work if you are having fun. That is what Kissing in the Kitchen: The Romantic Comedy Cookbook for Couples is all about, FUN! It's simple, couples who enjoy spending time together, spend time together (hmmm) – they look forward to it. The more fun times you share as a couple, the stronger the bond you will build. That's what I call building emotional capital.

News flash...

It's not "If", but "When..." The trials of life and marriage will set in. And, Yes, as a couple you have to have the strength and cohesion to weather those turbulent times together, but when the skies turn gray and the storm sets in, who do you want to be shut in with "Debbie or Dougie Downer" or "Phyllis or Phillip Fun-maker?" And... who do you think your spouse wants to be held up with? Relationship guru - Dr. Phil posed a question that he felt every married person should ask themselves, and I have to agree, **"How fun are you to live with?"** The answer to this question could mean the difference between enjoying a beautiful, loving relationship that lasts a lifetime or, well...not! Listen, fun is where you find it, or create it. But, if you need an invitation to have fun, here it is.

For more marriage and relation insights visit:
www.weddingministernow.com.

Content

Dinner and a movie… Who knew?

Cooking dinner… ~ Watching movies…

The Kissing in the Kitchen DIY System

How to use this cookbook/relationship building workbook

Movies and Recipes

Date Night

Potato Skins ~ Baked Lobster ~ Seafood Risotto

The Five Year Engagement

Eggs Benedict w/Lobster ~New York Strip

Julie and Julia

Mushroom Chicken ~ Pork Chops with Apple Dijon Sauce ~Classic Vodka Martini

Soul Food

Golden Fried Chicken ~ Cheesy Macaroni and Cheese ~ King's Greens

Sex and the City

Spaghetti with Meatballs ~ Caesar's Salad ~ Cosmopolitan

Think Like A Man

Eggs Florentine ~ Caprese Salad

This Is 40

Grilled Chicken ~ Grilled Corn

It's Complicated

Chicken Soup ~ Pesto Paste and Green Bean Salad ~ Baked Chicken

The Devil Wears Prada

Parmesan French Fries ~ Jarlsburg Cheese Toast

Guess Who

Pan Seared Chicken Fajitas ~ Fresh Lemonade

Meet the Fockers

Vegetable Frittata ~ Tom Collins

Jumping the Broom

Champagne Oysters on the Half ~ Chilled Shrimp ~ Mimosas

Quick Cooking Techniques

Find easy common cooking techniques

Couple's Guided Movie Discussions

Questions for couples from the University of Rochester study

Credits

Research credits

Cooking Method Credits

Movie Credits

This book is dedicated to my new husband L.C. Clark and to every newlywed and truly-wed who is willing to keep love fun!

Dinner and a movie... Who knew?

Say it again, "stronger, longer..."
You might ask, "Will this workbook really help me and my spouse build a stronger, longer relationship that will last a lifetime?" Which is, a very good question (my compliments to you). To that I say, "It can't hurt!" Kissing in the Kitchen: The Romantic Comedy Cookbook for Couples, offers your relationship the best of both worlds. If one is good, two should be great. Studies now report that both cooking together and watching RomComs have strong relationship building merits on their own as separate activities. It stands to reason, (don't you think?), that together not only will you have fun but the two of you should both strengthen and lengthen your relationship in the process.

As a newbie to the Marriage and Relationship Education community, I can't wait to hear what the experts have to say about this no-brainer idea of bringing these two powerhouse relationship building activities together in to one easy to maintain DIY(do-it-yourself) relationship building program.

So, who are some of these experts and what do they have to say about ...

Cooking dinner...
Dr. John Gray best known for his Men are from Mars, Women are from Venus book series reports that during a study he conducted he found that, 70% of the married couple's surveyed said they enjoyed cooking together. More to the point, those same couples also reported being significantly more satisfied in ALL areas of their lives than couples who don't cook together(Ashley Martell, October 29, 2014).

Here's why. According to Todd Foley of Focus on the Family – Canada (a repository of information dedicated to helping families stay stronger longer), "Relationship experts suggest couples use cooking as a way to invest in the marriage by intentionally spending time together." He goes on to cite licensed marriage therapist Sharon O'Neil author of *A Short Guide to a Happy Marriage* as saying , "Having a special time to look forward to helps sustain good feelings and promotes positive anticipatory emotions. Such behaviour shows that the couple is making their relationship a priority." It also shows that the couple is having fun!

Watching movies...
Ronald D. Rogge, PhD, Associate Professor of Psychology at the University of Rochester and his team report that newly-weds and truly-weds who watch romantic comedies together and discuss them, may have a **fifty-percent** better chance of staying together than couples who do not. Their study found that couples can watch RomComs together as an inexpensive yet effective method of couples' counseling. This little rabbit out of the researcher's hat, took everyone by surprise in 2014 and gained these innovative psychologists a lot of well-deserved attention from higher end news sources like the New York Times and USA Today. For more information about this study visit: http://www.rochester.edu/news/divorce-rate-cut-in-half-for-couples-who-discussed-relationship-movies/

The Kissing in the Kitchen DIY System

As I mentioned, this book is all about having fun, making positive investments in your relationship's emotional capital and making your marital bonds stronger so that your relationship will last longer. Whew, that is a mouthful. These are lofty goals to reach and no matter who gets involved, only you and your spouse can actually reach them. No one can do it for you. So with this being the case, you might as well start with a do-it-yourself mindset. This book provides a system, but you have to work it. Much like the recipes in this book, the results will only be as good as the effort.

How to use this cookbook/workbook

As a relationship building workbook
This is a simple yet fun and engaging 5 week, 3 step DIY relationship building program.

1. Pick a movie from the Content and choose a recipe to make as a couple. Choose a new movie each week for 5 weeks.

2. Prepare the recipe you like together. Watch the movie and enjoy the meal. **Note:** Just for fun, look for the 🎥 at the end of each recipe so that you know where you will see or hear about the dish you prepared in the movie.

3. Use the Couple's Guided Discussion questions on page 71 of this book to help you to thoroughly discuss each movie, or log on to the University of Rochester' study and use theirs.

   Additional features:
   I've included what I call "**Easy Answers**" at the end of most of the movie's recipes. Each **"Easy Answer"** is based on my personal experience, and always reinforces my basic belief that forgiveness, love, humility and good interpersonal communication skills form the foundation of a lasting relationship.

As a movie foodie cookbook
If you have not figured this out yet, all of the recipes in this cookbook are based on meals seen in the movies. I am a movie foodie from way back. I love, love, love food in movies and having the opportunity to share this love with you is so awesome. So anyway, to use this book as a cookbook, simply find a recipe and make it. Lol Bon appetite!

Stronger, longer...

Date Night (2010)

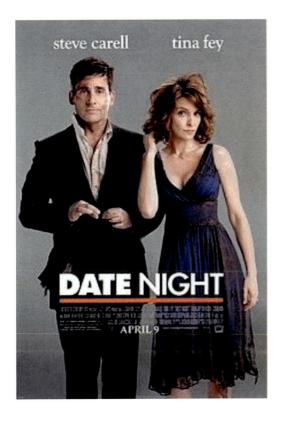

Written by Josh Klausner, Directed by Shawn Levy and Starring Steve Carell and Tina Fey.

Synopsis:
After spending time with friends whose marriage has hit the skids, Phil and Claire Foster begin to worry that they too are on the road to divorce. Complacency and predictability had all but replaced passion in their marriage. One crazy night of pulse racing, roof raising antics, and a deadly case of mistaken identity was enough to give their marriage a good shot of H2-us.

Date Night - Potato Skins

CAST & CREW: Mise en place

3 small to medium Yukon Gold potatoes
Vegetable oil
Kosher salt
Freshly ground pepper
2 strips of cooked bacon - crumbled
2 to 3 oz. cooked steak – your choice, I used leftover New York Strip - Cubed
2 to 3 oz. grated cheddar cheese
¼ cup sour cream
1 Garlic clove thinly sliced
2 green onions - thinly sliced

SCRIPT:

Preheat oven to 400 degrees.

Rub each potato all over with oil, and bake on a cookie sheet until done (about 30 min). Once done, remove from oven and allow cooling.

When cooled, cut them in half (the long way) and scoop out the center with a spoon. Leave about a 1/3 inch of potato in the skin. Set the scooped potatoes aside in a bowl. Increase the oven temperature to 450 degrees.

Now, brush all of the potatoes, inside and outside with oil and set on a baking rack, in a roasting pan not on a cookie sheet. Return to the oven. After about 10 minutes flip the skins over and allow to cook for an additional ten minutes.

While the skins are baking, mash the potatoes and season with salt and pepper. Stir in half of the bacon, steak, and cheese.

Stuff the skins with the mashed potato mix. Top with steak and cheese and scatter bacon and green onions. Set back in the oven for 5 or 6 minutes until cheese is melted. Serve hot with a dollop of sour cream.

Phil and Clair share this dish on their regular date night. Well a dish like this…these are amazing.

Date Night - Baked Lobster Tail

CAST & CREW: Mise en place

2 (6-ounce) Lobster Tails
2-4 tablespoons Melted Butter
1/2 teaspoons Lemon Zest
1/4 teaspoon Minced Garlic
1 tablespoon Chopped Parsley
Salt to taste

SCRIPT:

Preheat oven to 350 degrees.

Prep the Garlic Butter:
In a small sauce pan over medium heat, add 2 tablespoons butter, lemon zest, garlic and salt, allow melting slowly.

Next, piggy back the lobster tails: Using kitchen shears, cut down the center of the hard shell top. Do not cut into the fan portion of the tail. Now, flip over and press on each of the bottom ribs to break them, flip tail back over and run your thumb between the meat and the cut shell to separate them and then finally, pull the meat out and over the top of the cut shell.

Now, set the lobster tails in a baking dish and brush each lobster tail with butter mixture.

Bake for about 15 minutes until the temperature of each is 140 to 145 degrees.

Finally, remove tails from oven and slather once more with the butter sauce and scatter with the chopped parsley. Serve while hot.

🎥 When Clair and Phil go on the big date to the fancy restaurant, the couple behind them orders the lobster tail. Lol

Date Night – Seafood Risotto

CAST & CREW: Mise en place

Olive oil
2 medium shallots, finely diced
1 cup small bay scallops
1 lobster tail – separated into chunks by hand
¼ lb. shrimp -peeled, deveined and chopped
1 clove of garlic, peeled and minced
1 cup white wine
1 cup Arborio rice
1 pint chicken stock
2 tablespoons butter
Kosher salt and freshly ground black pepper
¼ cup chopped flat-leaf parsley

SCRIPT:

Seafood prep:
In a large sauté pan over high heat add one tablespoon of oil. Once oil is hot, add shallots and garlic and sauté until translucent -- about 3 minutes. Add seafood and sauté lightly until shrimp are red and tender. Add ½ cup of wine. Continue to cook over high heat until wine cooks down. Set seafood mixture aside.

Rice:
In a medium-sized pan add 2 tablespoons of olive oil and butter. Heat pan on medium heat. Add diced shallots and sweat until translucent. Add rice and stir to coat well with the oil. Add wine and stir until just about completely evaporated - for just a few moments.

Next, add one ladle of stock and allow it to absorb in to the rice, stir to avoid sticking. Continue to add stock one ladle at a time until the rice is tender but firm. Add salt and pepper to taste.

Next, add in the seafood mixture. Reserve a bit for the top. Garnish with the parsley.

 Phil and Clair actually order the Risotto at the fancy restaurant on their big date night.

How to Enjoy Your Marriage for the Rest of Your Life

By Interfaith minister Stacey Y. Moore

Appreciation is the golden key to joy. As time wears on we tend to grow accustomed and even bored with our lives and our surroundings. We can become unappreciative in many aspects of our lives. Sometimes that includes our relationships with our spouses. This is no criminal offense, but it is avoidable. To enjoy your marriage for the rest of your life you will have to **adopt an attitude of gratitude!**

When you begin to feel as if you are missing out on something, take stock of what you have. Gaze on your life with new eyes and imagine what someone who does not have everything that you have, would think of your life. Allow yourself to feel appreciative for what you have and for all that you will have. Allow yourself to take pride in the life that you are creating with your spouse.

Here are a few tips

1. Focus on your own garden and forget how green the grass seems on the other side. Things may look good from the window, but when you look closer you may find that they are not as great as you think.
2. Take an emotional journey with your spouse down memory lane. Focus on the love that brought you together. Make a big deal of it with dinner and dancing… because you are really cool like that!
3. For five days strait, wake up and before you get out of bed, allow yourself to feel thankful for everything you can think of: Your health, home, family, friends etc…

Your turn - List some things that you are truly appreciative for?

"It is not a lack of love, but a lack of friendship that makes unhappy marriages."

— *Friedrich Nietzsche*

The Five Year Engagement (2012)

Written by Jason Segel, Nicholas Stoller, Directed by Nicholas Stoller. Starring Jason Segel, and Emily Blunt.

Synopsis:
Tom and Violet, a perfect couple, that was meant-to-be, almost wasn't because they were waiting for the perfect time to have the perfect wedding. What they didn't know is that life will get in the way if you let it and that, there is no perfect time, only now!

The Five Year Engagement - Eggs Benedict with Lobster

CAST & CREW: Mise en place

Sandwich:
2 fresh eggs
1 tablespoon white vinegar
½ cup Hollandaise Sauce
2 grilled Ciabatta Roll bottoms or tops, your choice
2 slices really nice Canadian bacon
½ cup lobster tail meat – cooked and hand separated/ can be replaced with crab meat
2 tablespoons chopped parsley, for garnish

SCRIPT:

Begin by heating up the hollandaise sauce and set aside.

Now, place bacon in a non-stick sauté pan over medium heat to warm. Once warmed, place a slice of bacon on each half of Grilled Ciabatta. Keep warm in a low heated oven

Now poach the eggs (see techniques) in the back on the book in the Techniques section.

Place poached eggs atop the bacon,

Scatter the lobster on both sandwiches

Top with hollandaise sauce. Garnish with parsley.

Roasted Asparagus – CAST & CREW
6 to 8 Asparagus Spears – Cleaned and trimmed – Cut off the woody bottoms
1 clove Garlic – Sliced thin
Olive oil
Salt and fresh ground Pepper

SCRIPT:

Preheat oven to 400 degrees. Place all of the asparagus spears and garlic slices on a cookie sheet and drizzle with oil. Salt and pepper them to taste. Toss to make sure all are covered. Pop in to oven for about 10 minutes.

Tom makes this totally delish breakfast for Violet the morning after their engagement and serves it with a little moon pie. Ha ha ha!

The Five Year Engagement - New York Strip

CAST & CREW: Mise en place

2 New York Strip steaks 1-inch thick
Canola oil
Kosher salt and freshly ground black pepper
1 clove of garlic, peeled and bashed
1 sprig of thyme

Pan Sauce:
2 tablespoons finely diced shallots

1 clove of garlic, peeled and minced
1/4 cup red wine
1/2 cup low-sodium beef stock
A pinch of lemon zest
1 tablespoons butter - cold

SCRIPT:

Dry steaks with a paper towel, salt and pepper them and set aside. Next, heat 3 tablespoons of oil over medium-high heat in a large fry pan. Add steaks and cook for 2-3 minutes until you have a nice sear on the steak.

Now, with a large spoon baste the steaks with pan juice. You may need to tilt the pan. Add thyme and garlic and continue to baste and cook for 7-8 minutes.

Remove steaks and allow resting on a plate.

Next, reduce the heat and retain all but a tablespoon of the oil in the pan.

Next, sauté the shallots and garlic until they are translucent. Add wine and allow it to reduce. Add the stock and lemon zest. Let the sauce simmer and reduce further.

Once it has thickened a bit, add cold butter and move around in the pan to thicken more. Season to taste with salt and fresh ground pepper.

Serve with baked potatoes, roasted asparagus and a salad.

 In the final scene, Violet prepares this meal for Tom, and it ain't half bad.

Julie and Julia (2009)

Written and directed by Nora Ephron starring Meryl Streep, Stanley Tucci, Amy Adams, and Chris Messina.

Synopsis:
Newlywed, Julie Powell is underwhelmed with her life and sets out to prove her self-worth by recreating all 524 of Julia Childs' French recipes and by blogging about it for one strait year. During this time her new husband Eric is unwittingly forced into a supporting role. In parallel, the movie also chronicles the love story of truly-weds Julia Child and her husband Paul.

Julie and Julia – Mushroom Chicken

CAST & CREW: Mise en place

4 chicken breasts or thighs boneless
2 tablespoons canola oil
½ teaspoon lemon juice, fresh
5 tablespoons butter
1 tablespoon shallots, minced
¼ lb. button mushrooms, sliced
Salt and pepper

SAUCE
¼ cup chicken stock
¼ cup sherry

1 cup whipping cream

Salt and pepper to taste
2 tablespoons Italian parsley, chopped
1 sprig of rosemary - chopped

SCRIPT:

Start by preheating oven to 400 degrees. Next, rub lemon juice all over the chicken and season with salt and pepper. Now, warm a fry pan over medium heat and add 2 tablespoons of oil.

Once oil is warm, add the chicken to the oil, skin side down. Allow to fry until golden brown. Flip over and continue to cook for 5 minutes.

Remove from the oil to a baking dish, skin side up and set in the oven. Allow to bake for about 20 minutes or until fully done. It is done when the juices run clear when you poke it with a fork.

Next, create the sauce. Drain off most of the oil left in the fry pan, leaving about a tablespoon. Warm over medium to low heat, add butter and allow melting. Using a wooden spoon mix the butter with the pan juices.

Next, add the shallots, mushroom and rosemary. Season with salt and pepper and sauté without browning. As the pan juice begins to cook down, add the sherry. Raise the heat and allow the sherry to reduce. Stir often.

Once the sherry has reduces, add the stock and bring to a boil, stir in the cream and add the parsley. Allow to simmer on low heat until the chicken is done.

Finally, remove the chicken from the oven, place pieces on a serving plate and pour the mushroom cream sauce over them and serve.

See this dish early in the film; Julie prepares it as a second dish for her blog. Remember, "Don't crowd the mushrooms." This one is my own interpretation. I like crispy chicken. Lol

Julie and Julia - Pork Chops with Apple Dijon Sauce

CAST & CREW: Mise en place

4 pork chops
Olive oil
½ onion - thinly sliced
1 clove garlic, sliced
2-3 Sprigs fresh sage – tear the leaves
2 tablespoons Dijon mustard
2 tablespoons honey
¼ teaspoon Allspice
1 ½ cups unfiltered apple juice
1 small granny smith apple - cored and cut into thin slices
2 tablespoons butter, cold
Sea salt and freshly ground black pepper

SCRIPT:

Start by coating the pork chops with olive oil and season with salt and pepper to taste.

Next, sear in a heavy pan over high heat for about 6 minutes on each side. Remove and set aside on a plate.

Next, in the same pan add your onions, garlic and sage leaves. Sauté them for about 3 minutes.

Now, add the mustard, apples, honey and allspice. Mix well and pour in the apple juice. Reduce the heat and allow it to simmer over lower heat until apples are tender but still firm (check with a fork). You don't want to overcook the apples.

Now, use a slotted spoon to remove the apples and put them on top of the Pork chops.

Add cold butter to the pan sauce and stir it well. It will thicken. Be sure to taste. You may want to add more honey. Add salt and pepper to taste. Pour over the chops.

See this dish when Julie meets with a New York Times reporter. She serves it with, spinach and mashed potatoes. Also, she only uses a Dijon sauce with no apples. I like apples, so I shared apples. Hope you like them too.

Julie and Julia – Vodka Martini

CAST & CREW: Mise en place

4 oz. chilled Vodka
2 teaspoons Dry Vermouth
2 green olives
A twist of lemon peel
Ice

SCRIPT:

In a cocktail shaker, pour the Vodka and Dry Vermouth.

Add ice and shake well.

Use a strainer and pour martinis into a frosted martini glasses.

Drop the olives into the martinis. Finish by arranging a twist of lemon peel on the rim of the glass.

Julie and Pete enjoy martinis while they watch Julia cook on television. They gloss over it quickly so look hard.

How to negotiate harmoniously in your marriage

By Interfaith minister Stacey Y. Moore

Have you ever heard the old saying, "You have to pick your battles?" It's true, not everything is worth the energy it takes to debate it. Debate is code for argue or have a temper tantrum. Just kidding. I know that you are way too evolved to argue or fall out on the floor screaming. Anyway, to the point, once you find that there is a real need for a grown up discussion about a particular subject, issue, need or want, it is time to take it to the negotiation table. As grownups I would hope that you both remember that being strong is not the same thing as being tough. While there is lots of room at the table for a strong and healthy negotiation; there is absolutely no room in negotiations for tough guy/gal tactics. Not at home, not anywhere.

Let the Negotiations begin!

- **Sit on the same side of the table.** No matter what you are still a team, sitting on opposite sides of the table (like above) is like drawing a line and each of you stepping on a different sides of it to protect your position. It is warlike and not at all conducive to harmony in negotiations.

- **Make sure that you are on the same page.** As much as we would like to think that we are good communicators, many times the people closest to us, have no idea what we are really talking about. Before you begin your negotiations, make sure that both of you are clear about what the real issue is. Both of you should verbalize the issue aloud to be sure that you are in agreement.

- **Write down your pros and cons .** Each of you should take the time to internalize your thoughts and to fully grasp the situation. Each of you should make a good old fashioned Ben Franklin list with one side of the paper dedicated to the **Pros (positive aspects)** of the situation and one side to the **Cons (negative aspects)** of the situation.

- **Be ready to give something in exchange for what you want.** It is only a win - win if everyone wins. If you are negotiating for something specific, the other person should also receive something that they want. However, make sure that all bounties are equitable. No one will be happy in the long run if they accept an unfair deal to get what they need or want in the short run. It's like getting a credit card with a really high interest rate.
- ; the fun is over but the dues you pay can last a long time.

- **Celebrate the resolution.** Whatever your pleasure, be ready to toast to the successful resolution of your negotiations. This gets you ready for a positive outcome by setting the expectation that you will drink the sparkling cider or if you are me, Champagne.

Your turn -What do you need to negotiate with your spouse?

_____

_____

_____

_____

_____

_____

_____

_____

All enduring success is founded upon harmonious human relationships.
— Napoleon Hill

"The more connections you and your lover make, not just between your bodies, but between your minds, your hearts, and your souls, the more you will strengthen the fabric of your relationship, and the more real moments you will experience together."

— *Barbara De Angelis*

Soul Food (1997)

Written and Directed by: George Tillman Jr. Stars: Vanessa Williams, Vivica A. Fox, Nia Long, Michael Beach, Mekhi Phifer, Brandon Hammon and Jeffrey D. Sams.

Synopsis:
A mid-west family with newlyweds, truly-weds and why-did-we-weds, shares the story of their triumphs, failures and the bonds that ultimate keep real families together.

Soul Food – Home Style Fried Chicken

CAST & CREW: Mise en place

1 whole (cut up) frying chicken
1 ½ tsp. Seasoned Salt
½ tsp. black pepper to taste
½ tsp. garlic powder
½ tsp. onion powder
1 cups flour in a large paper bag
1 to 2 cups of shortening or if you want to go the healthy route 2 cups vegetable oil.

SCRIPT:

First our main character (you) adds the dry seasonings to the flour, closes the bag and shakes it up well.

Next, rinse and dry the chicken pieces well with a paper towel. Fold the chicken wing tips in and under the drumstick part. Now shake the chicken in the bag until fully coated. Set aside until oil is hot. Next over medium high/heat in a cast iron or heavy bottom fry pan, heat your shortening or oil. Test by putting the end of a wooden spoon in the oil to see if it's hot.

Once the oil is hot, start by putting in the thighs (skin side down) and legs and wings. Reduce the heat to medium. Cook for 6 minutes then turn over with a fork. Now add the breasts. Put a lid on top and allow cooking for 10 minutes then turning over again replace lid. Cook for 10 minutes and turn again. Keep the lid off and cook on each side until golden brown and crispy.

Poke with your fork to make sure all juices are running clear. Remove chicken and set on a paper towel covered plate to drain the oil.

See this dish in the family dinner scenes. Like many of the other meals in this movie, you will actually see the preparation. Use my recipe instead! Lol

Soul Food – Cheesy Macaroni and Cheese

CAST & CREW: Mise en place

1 bag medium elbow macaroni
1 stick. salted or unsalted butter
¼ cup all-purpose flour
4 cups hot half and half
1 tsp. kosher salt
½ tsp. freshly ground black pepper
Pinch nutmeg
4 cups Gruyere cheese, grated
4 cups Cheddar Cheese grated
Salt

SCRIPT:
First, bring a large pot of water to a boil. Add a dash of salt and pour in the macaroni. Stir to separate the pasta and allow cooking until tender. Once the pasta is tender, drain, rinse with cold water and set aside.

Next, in a medium sized pot, over low heat, warm the half and half slowly. Do not burn or allow boiling. Now, melt the butter slowly over low heat in a saucepan and add the flour all at once, stirring with a wooden spoon for 2 minutes. Next, slowly pour the hot half and half into the butter–flour mixture and simmer, whisking constantly, until the sauce is thickened and smooth.

Next, remove from heat and add the salt, pepper, nutmeg, ½ of the cheeses. Mix well and pour over the pasta. Coat the pasta well by stirring.

Finally, pour the pasta into a baking dish or 6-8 small dishes if being served as an appetizer. Top with the rest of the cheese and bake at 400 until golden brown. Serve while still hot.

🎥 You won't see this dish because Hitch only talks about making it before he and Sara have a big fight.

Soul Food – King's Greens

CAST & CREW: Mise en place

1 bunch of Collard Greens
2 tablespoons olive oil
1 portion - Mira Poix (see Quick Cooking Techniques)
1 medium ham hock
2 tablespoons white vinegar
Seasoned salt
½ cube of Knorr Chicken bouillon
Fresh ground black pepper
2 garlic cloves
Salt if needed

SCRIPT:

Cook the ham hock: In a medium sized boiler over medium-high heat warm the olive oil. Add the mire poix and sauté for 3 minutes. Fill the pot ¾ full with water and bring to a boil. Add seasoned salt and pepper. Add the ham hock and reduce the heat to medium high. Cover with a lid and allow cooking for about 1 ½ hours. Add more water if necessary. Cook until the meat is tender and falls off the bone. Once the ham hock is tender add the bouillon and vinegar. Allow to simmer a minute or two.

Clean the Greens 3 times.
Fill an empty, clean sink with cold water. Submerge the greens and allow sitting for about 2 minutes. Swish the greens around and remove. Allow all of the water to drain. Clean out the sink again and fill with water again. This time add about 2 tbsp. of salt. Submerge the greens and swish them vigorously. Remove the greens, clean the sink and do it one more time. Trim the rough ends from the greens and remove any yellow ones.

Cook the Greens: Layer 3 or 4 leaves, one atop another and roll them like a cigar then cut into 1 inch thick rounds and set aside in a bowl. Add the garlic to the ham hock, and allow to cook for 5 minutes. Add the greens and put a lid on the pot. Cook for 45 minutes. Cook for another 25 minutes.

🎥 In the movie, you can actually see a demo on the preparation of this dish.

HOW TO FORGIVE THE UNFORGIVEABLE
By Interfaith minister Stacey Y. Moore

Let me start by saying that there is nothing that can be done that cannot be forgiven. In the words of Princess Elsa of Walt Disney's Frozen, **"Let it go, let it go, it doesn't matter anymore!"** Forgiving is freedom. Only you have the power to free yourself from your memories of past hurts.

Is pain your comfort zone?
Letting go seems like a very hard thing to do because it takes a lot of courage to free yourself from painful memories. In fact the pain that fuels a continuous grudge actually can become a comfort zone. After all if we forgive and let go of the pain, we may forget and somehow allow the person or situation that caused the pain (to our ego) to do it again. So rather than freeing ourselves, we don't want to take the risk of having our egos knocked down a peg or two once more. What we don't consider is that holding on to that pain at this point may just be a bad habit.

Forgive and move on!
Author and Life Coach Iyanla Vanzant , In her new book, [FORGIVENESS: 21 Days to Forgive Everyone for Everything](), says that , "Forgiveness inevitably leads to acceptance. It is a demonstration of your willingness to move on." In essence, if you are unable to forgive, you will be unable to move forward. You are sentencing yourself to spend your life in the hell of your past. The other thing to note here is that, just like you are the only one who can feel it if you get pinched on the arm, you are also the only one feeling the pain of any resentments, anger or sadness you harbor. You are at this point, hurting yourself.

Face your fear!
To forgive, you will have to allow yourself to be courageous. Simply face your fear head on. Take a deep breath and with your exhale, let it go! The past cannot hurt you anymore.

Your turn – What do you need to forgive today?

_____

_____

_____

_____

"The weak can never forgive. Forgiveness is the attribute of the strong."
— Mahatma Gandhi, *All Men are Brothers: Autobiographical Reflections*

"In the process of planning and having a wedding, I forgot there would actually be a marriage, a union of minds, bodies, souls, and issues that would come together as soon as the ceremony was over."

*Iyanla Vanzant, Peace from Broken Pieces:
How to Get Through What You're Going Through*

Sex and the City (2008)

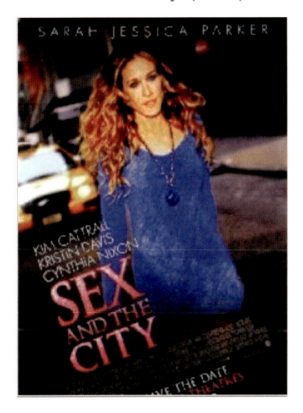

Written and Directed by Michael Patrick King. Starring Sarah Jessica Parker, Kim Cattrall, Kristin Davis, Cynthia Nixon.

Synopsis:
This is an amazing movie reprise of the runaway hit television show featuring the four most famous New Yorkers in the world. In the movie, our girl Carrie is finally gonna marry Big. That is until she becomes more concerned with the wedding than the marriage. Hearts are broken, friendships are tested, and lessons are learned.

Sex and the City - Spaghetti with Meatballs

CAST & CREW: Mise en place

Meatballs:
1 lb. ground beef or ground turkey,
1 ½ cup fresh homemade French bread croutons - crumbled
1 tablespoon fresh parsley – fine chopped
1 tablespoon fresh thyme – leaves only
2 garlic cloves – chopped fine
¼ cup heavy cream
Salt and fresh ground pepper – generously
3 tablespoons canola oil

Sauce:
¼ cup olive oil
1 medium onion - chopped fine
5 garlic cloves – chopped fine
2 bay leaves
8 Roma tomatoes - peeled and quartered - (see Quick Cooking Techniques for recipe)
¼ cup white wine
1 (6 oz.) can tomato paste
Salt and pepper to taste
1 teaspoon sugar
3-4 sprigs fresh basil - torn
3-4 sprigs fresh parsley - chopped
¼ teaspoon red pepper flakes
1 lb. spaghetti

SCRIPT:

Sauce: In a large pan add the olive oil and heat over medium heat. Add the onions, stir for 1 minute and add the garlic and bay leaves. Allow to simmer and add in the Tomatoes, stir. Add in the tomato paste and stir well. Add the wine, sugar and parsley. Stir well, Cover the top and reduce the heat. Simmer low for 45 min. to 1 hour.

Meat Balls: In a large bowl mix together all of the meatball ingredients. Chill in the refrigerator for an hour. Remove from refrigerator and roll dollops of the mix into golf ball sized balls. Set on a plate. Next, heat a large fry pan and add canola oil. Once heated add the meat balls. Do not crowd the pan. Brown each ball on all sides. Add the meat ball to the sauce and cover the sauce.

Spaghetti: Bring a large pot of water to a boil. Add a dash of salt. Add spaghetti noodles. Stir occasionally to make sure they don't stick. When tender, drain and toss with a little olive oil. Plate pasta and top with sauce and meatballs.

This recipe will yield leftovers. You are welcome!

Sex and the City - Caesar's Salad

CAST & CREW: Mise en place

Dressing:
1 tablespoon Anchovy paste
1½ cups of mayonnaise – (see Quick Cooking Techniques for recipe)
1 whole lemon – juiced
1 whole garlic clove
Salt and pepper to taste

Salad:
1 head Romaine lettuce heart – Cleaned, cut and dried
½ cup French bread croutons – Homemade
¼ cup Parmesan cheese - shredded

SCRIPT:

Add all of the dressing ingredients into a blender and pulse until thoroughly mixed.

In a large bowl, toss the lettuce with the dressing. Next, add the croutons and half the cheese and toss again. Serve the salad in two bowls and top with more cheese.

Both the spaghetti and the Caesar's salad can be seen in the "dinner out" scene with Miranda, Steve, Magda and Brady. Miranda and Steve get into a tiff while little Brady digs in. He makes the spaghetti look so good.

Sex and the City – Cosmopolitan

CAST & CREW: Mise en place

2 oz. Grey Goose vodka
1 oz. triple sec
1 oz. fresh lime juice
1 oz. cranberry juice

SCRIPT:

Shake vodka, triple sec, lime and cranberry juice vigorously in a shaker with lots of ice.

Strain into a sexy martini glass, garnish with a lime wedge on the rim, an orange curl or a cherry, and serve.

🎥 The girls revisit this oldie but goodie at the end of the film. Don't worry guys, it is okay to have this drink in the privacy of your own home. Real men drink Cosmos. Lol

HOW TO KEEP THE CONNECTION, ONCE YOU HAVE KIDS

By Interfaith minister Stacey y. Moore

It takes planning and commitment to keep a strong connection between a husband and wife. As much as I hate to admit it, when our children entered the picture, my energy level seemed to exit. As a working mother and wife, once I came home, cooked dinner and picked up the house (my second shift) I was too tired to focus on my husband and that was even when he helped. Over time, it became the norm and after a while, we both started to feel disconnected. While having fun family outing (when the kids were old enough) definitely helped us to bond as a family unit, they did not do much to help my husband and I bond as a couple. So here is what I learned and what I suggest you do if you find you need to re-connect.

Here is a list of ideas to help you keep your own connection strong!

1. **Plan to have dinner alone, as a couple at least two to three times a week**. This could mean feeding the kids first and putting them to bed. A date night is a good idea. Try to make it fun for the kids so that they will look forward to your date night as well.

2. **Share the responsibility of taking care of the children as equitably as possible**. This is a real point of contention in many marriages. One parent is saddled with the day to day and even night to night care of the kids while the other goes to work and comes home. It's not fair! Work this out early so that you are shouldering the responsibility as a cohesive couple.

3. **Always make the children sleep in their own bed.** This can be a hard one but if you spend a little time with them in their room until they falloff to sleep, they will be more comfortable in their own space. Make it fun for them, play a game with them or read to them regularly just before bed.

4. **Get the kids on a regular bedtime schedule.** This may be hard at first but in the long run, it will be the gift that keeps on giving. You just have to be strong to and keep the schedule going.

5. **Teach your children healthy boundaries early**. I don't believe in closed doors, but if a door is closed, everyone should know to knock and await an invitation to enter before opening the door. This will save you many embarrassing moments.

6. **As parents, never discuss grown up issues in earshot of your children.** This is from firsthand experience; your kids will embarrass you at the worst time possible. They soak up everything and tell everything. Everything!

Your turn - What can you do to help keep the connection with your spouse?

_____

_____

_____

_____

_____

_____

_____

"HAPPINESS [is] ONLY REAL WHEN SHARED"
— Jon Krakauer, Into the Wild

Think Like A Man (2012)

Directed by Tim Story, Writers: Keith Merryman (screenplay), David A. Newman (screenplay). Stars: Gabrielle Union, Kevin Hart, Michael Ealy, Jerry Ferrara, Meagan Good, Regina Hall, Taraji P. Henson, Terrence Jenkins, Romany Malco, Gary Owen and Wendy Williams and Chris Brown.

Synopsis:
With an amazingly talented ensemble cast, this funny he-said/ she-said movie sets out to prove that in the war between the sexes, there are no winners and no losers because there is no war, only insecurities.

Think Like A Man - Eggs Florentine

CAST & CREW: Mise en place

Eggs:
2 fresh eggs
1 tablespoon white vinegar
1 cup Hollandaise sauce:
(see Quick Cooking Techniques for recipe)
4 slices Canadian bacon sliced into thin ribbons
1 cup of Fresh spinach – sautéed and wilted
2 large slices of beefsteak tomato
2 Ciabatta rolls, split in half and grilled
2 tablespoons chopped chives, for garnish

SCRIPT:

Begin the poaching process. (see Quick Cooking Techniques for recipe)

Meanwhile, grill the rolls on a stove top grill, until light brown on cut side. Flip over then reduce heat to keep warm. Place tomato slices on top of each bottom. Top the tomato with spinach.

Place bacon in a non-stick pan over medium heat to warm. Be careful not to overcook because it will dry out. – You are only warming it!

Now poach the eggs. (see Quick Cooking Techniques for recipe)

Place 1 egg on each half of grilled roll, pour 1/4 of a cup of hollandaise sauce over the top of each egg. Pile on the bacon ribbons and garnish with finely chopped chives.

This little hot number is served up as the morning after, breakfast-in-bed meal when Dominic shows Lauren just how tasty good love making can be. I don't know ,but this may be an opportunity meal for the fellas to prepare for the ladies... I 'm just sayin

Think Like A Man – Caprese Salad

CAST & CREW: Mise en place

1 large ripe tomato, sliced 1/4 inch thick
1/4 pound fresh mozzarella cheese, sliced 1/4 inch thick rounds
1/3 cup fresh basil leaves
1-2 tablespoons extra virgin olive oil
2 tablespoons red wine vinegar
Sea salt to taste
Fresh ground black pepper to taste

SCRIPT:

On a plate, arrange the tomato slices, cheese and basil leaves, alternately and overlapping. Drizzle with olive oil and then the vinegar. Season to taste with salt and pepper.

🎥 Kristin serves Jeremy this dish when she is trying to get him to get a better job. Lol, I don't know if a little cheese is enough ladies. You may need a lot of wine with that cheese.

How to Lovingly Communicate with your Spouse

By Interfaith minister Stacey y. Moore

Loving communication is the key to a happy marriage. When most people hear the word communicate, they think talk. Communication is far more than one person spewing out a litany of words. As a matter of fact words are the least effective way that we as humans have to communicate love. It stands to reason that, if you are relying on just the right words to make a point or to resolve an issue, you will find it incredibly difficult to do so.

Listen up
To communicate lovingly with your spouse (and anyone else for that matter) requires less talk and more listening. And, if you think finding the right words is hard wait till you start listening for them. The right words are all of the words your loved one shares with you to convey to you their needs, wants, dreams, hopes, fears and desires (this is a short list). Basically anything that affects them in anyway is what you need to know about.

Act like you love em
What you do with the information your loved one shares with you, is what they will interpret as love, or not love. For example: if your husband says that he loves hot cocoa on cold nights and you make it your business to have hot cocoa in the winter time; your actions communicated love. If you tell your mate that you love daisies and you come home one day to find daisies planted in your front yard. That is an act that communicates love. You see where I am going here? Yes, yes, yes! **Actions speak louder than words when love is the language.**

I have to tell you… this does take practice. Most people are not good at doing rather than telling. But, you will see; doing is better. Your spouse (once they get it and they will get it) will let you know.

In summary!

- **Shhhh, stop talking!** Enough with the I love Yous; Prove it!

- **Listen up**- Listen to your spouse and take mental notes of the things that they report as having a specific effect on them, both positive and negative.

- **Act on it** -Put your love into action and give them what they love, and spare them what they don't love.

Your turn - What does your spouse love and what does your spouse hate?

_____
_____
_____
_____
_____
_____
_____
_____

> "Happily ever after is not a fairy tale. It's a choice."
> —Fawn Weaver

"The success of a relationship is a function of the extent to which it meets the needs of two people,"

Dr. Phil

This Is 40 (2012)

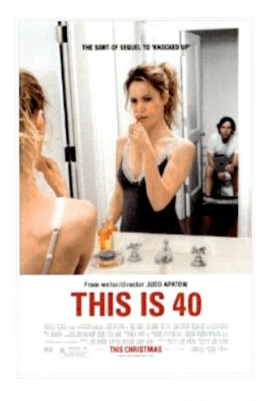

Written and Directed by Judd Apatow. With Paul Rudd, Leslie Mann, Maude Apatow, Iris Apatow.

Synopsis:
Thirty-nine year olds Pete and Debbie both feel the sharp teeth of "forty" nipping at their tail feathers but, each has their own way of working through their personal expectations about what that means. Debbie goes for health while Pete goes for his dreams, to the exclusion of health.

This is 40 – Roasted Corn on the Cobb

CAST & CREW: Mise en place

2 ears fresh corn on the cob – Husked, cleaned and dried
Olive oil
Salt and pepper to taste
¼ cup hollandaise sauce or mayonnaise – (see Quick Cooking Techniques for recipe)
¼ cup finely crumbled Feta cheese
¼ teaspoon smoked paprika powder
1 tablespoon finely chopped parsley
½ lime - cut into wedges

SCRIPT:

Heat grill to high heat.

Drizzle corn with olive oil all around. Season it with salt and pepper. Grill corn on each side until lightly charred.

Remove from grill and quickly cover with hollandaise or mayonnaise. Sprinkle with paprika and feta and top with parsley.

Finish with a squeeze of fresh lime juice.

This amazing roasted corn can be spotted at Pete's birthday party. This dish is so good. Be sure to eat it while it is hot.

This is 40 – Tangy Grilled Chicken

CAST & CREW: Mise en place

A whole chicken cut into parts – you can also use skinless chicken breasts for a heathier option.

Marinade:
6 tablespoons prepared Dijon mustard
3 cloves garlic, minced
2 green onions cut in half
3 tablespoons lime juice
4 ½ teaspoons lemon juice
¼ cup brown sugar
½ teaspoon salt
¼ teaspoon black pepper
1 teaspoon liquid smoke - mesquite
3 tablespoons olive oil

SCRIPT:

Mix together all of the marinades ingredients. Place the chicken parts into a large Ziploc bag. Pour marinade over chicken and massage to make sure all of the chicken is covered with the marinade. Refrigerate chicken in marinade for at least 8 hours, the longer the better.

Grill chicken until done, approximately 30 minutes. The chicken is done when the internal temperature of the thickest part reaches 160 degrees. Dark meat will take longer than the white meat so if you have a small grill, grill the thighs, legs and wings first, then the breasts.

🎥 A heathier, skinless version of this tangy, crispy, grilled chicken can be seen at Pete's 40th birthday party. I like crunchy chicken but if health is your thing (it really should be mine) then use the breasts instead.

TEN THINGS MARRIED PEOPLE SHOULD NEVER DO

BY INTERFAITH MINISTER STACEY Y. MOORE

While there may be a million ways to do most things; there are without any doubt certain things that married people should never do if they plan to stay married. In sitcoms like Everybody Loves Raymond and The King of Queens we watch as lovable crackpot husbands do the unthinkable to their disgruntled but accepting wives. Make these shows your go to classroom for what not to do. Always keep in mind that your spouse is like every other human who is not married to you, and he or she deserves your respect, loyalty and concern more than anyone else.

With that said… here is a list of things married people should never do to each other.

1. **Never share secrets entrusted in you by your spouse** – This is a big one. Know that trust is what you risk when you gossip about your spouse. Ask yourself if it is worth the loss. Once trust is broken is it slow to mend.

2. **Never talk down to your spouse in public** – Speaking to your spouse in a disrespectful way in public is unacceptable. Never treat your spouse in a way you would not approve of from others. People treat your stuff the way you treat your stuff (spouses included).

3. **Never become physical with your spouse** – If you are in a heated debate and are feeling like punching, shoving or scratching… don't do it. Walk away! Once a physical altercation starts; you cannot take it back. No one will forget and in most states it is illegal, and both of you could go to jail.

4. **Never tell non- professionals what goes on in your bedroom** – It is as simple as this… you are grown. It is no one else's business what goes on in your bedroom.

5. **Never tell others how much money your spouse earns** – Again, this is simple. You are grown and no one else needs to know your family's business.

6. **Never demand more from your spouse than you yourself are willing to give!** It's just not fair.

7. **Never plan a vacation that does not include your spouse without your spouse's permission.** A no brainer!

8. **Never open a new line of credit without your spouse's knowledge.** You know why!

9. **Never buy a new house without your spouse's input.** Again, you know why!

10. **Never tell your spouse your best friend's personal business** – When they are mad at you or your friend, it will come out. Blabber mouth.

Your turn - What are a few things you know you should quit doing to your spouse?

_____
_____
_____
_____
_____
_____
_____
_____

"To find someone who will love you for no reason, and to shower that person with reasons, that is the ultimate happiness."

-Robert Brault

It's Complicated (1999)

Written and directed by Nancy Meyers. Starring Meryl Streep, Steve Martin, Alec Baldwin, John Krasinski.

Synopsis:
Jane and Jake are divorced but, when their youngest child graduates from college a very unlikely and unexpected affair is launched. Old feelings come up and new revelations are made.

It's Complicated – Chicken Soup

CAST & CREW: Mise en place
2 qts. chicken broth: (see Quick Cooking Techniques for recipe)
4 chicken thighs or 2 breasts, skinless
2 tablespoons extra-virgin olive oil
½ large onion, diced
1-2 cloves garlic, crushed
4 small carrots - peel and cut on the angle in chunks
3 celery stalks, sliced on a bias
1 bay leaf
4 sprigs fresh thyme
A pinch of dried red pepper flakes

2 cups bowtie pasta
Kosher salt and freshly ground
Black pepper
Celery leaves for garnish
¼ cup finely grated parmesan cheese, for garnish

SCRIPT:

Warm a large stock pot over medium heat, add chicken broth and thighs and bring to a simmer to poach the meat -- approximately 20 minutes. When done, remove chicken and shred into medium-sized pieces. Reserve chicken broth.

Heat another large pot over medium-high heat and add olive oil, onions, celery, carrots and garlic. Sauté until translucent, about three minutes then add thyme, bay leaf and chili flakes.

Next, use a ladle and ladle in the chicken broth and bring to a simmer. Remove the bay leaves.

Add bowtie pasta and cook for 8-10 minutes until tender.

Taste for seasoning. Serve by ladling soup into the bowl, then top with shredded chicken and garnish with celery leaves and grated parmesan.

When Jake almost has a heart attack in a hotel room; instead of an afternoon of hot and steamy sex, the reunited couple enjoys a bowl of hot soup.

It's Complicated ~ Green Bean Pesto Salad

CAST & CREW: Mise en place

2 ½ cups cooked thin penne pasta
2 cups green beans
1 cup halved mini heirloom tomatoes
1 cup chopped Parsley
4 cloves minced roasted garlic
½ cup sliced Baby Bella mushrooms
¼ cup olive oil
Salt and pepper
¼ cup white wine vinegar
½ cup Pine nuts
6 Basil leaves
¼ cup chopped Italian Parsley
¼ cup Fresh Parmesan Cheese grated
1 tbsp. Dijon Mustard
1 tbsp. honey

SCRIPT:

Cook the Pasta: Bring a large pot of water to a boil. Season the water with salt. Add the pasta and allow to cook until tender, about 3-4 minutes. Drain and set aside.

Dressing: In a blender add the Basil, Parsley, Pine nuts, mustard, garlic, honey, white wine vinegar, Olive oil, salt and pepper and pulse until mixed. Set aside.

Vegetables: Warm a small amount of olive oil over a medium heat in a large skillet. Braise the green beans until tender then add the mushrooms. Add tomatoes last. Toss in oil, add salt and pepper to taste.

Combine: Add the pasta to the vegetable pan and mix together. Pour the pesto sauce over the pasta mixture. Coat all of the pasta and vegetables well. Serve warm or cold.

🎥 This dish can be seen during a family meal seen with Jane and the kids after Jake stands Jane up.

It's Complicated~ French Country Style Baked Chicken

CAST & CREW: Mise en place

1 large baking chicken
2 lemons cut in to quarters
3 sprigs of fresh thyme
2 sprigs of fresh sage
2 garlic bulbs, cut in half
Salt and pepper
2 tbsp. butter, melted
1 large white onion - quartered
1 stalk of celery cut into 4 large pieces
1 fresh bay leaf
1 tsp. olive oil

SCRIPT:

First, pre-heat your oven to 400 degrees. Now, pat dry your chicken and set in your roasting pan.

Liberally season the cavity of your chicken with salt and pepper. Next, in a bowl, toss together your: 4 pieces of lemon, 2 onions quarters, 2 garlic halves, celery and herbs. Season with salt and pepper.

Now, stuff the cavity of the bird with the fresh citrus mix. Tress the legs closed with cooking twine. Toss the extra lemon, onion and garlic in the pan around the chicken.

Coat the whole bird with the olive oil and salt and pepper well. Loosely cover top with tin foil.

Bake for 1 hour. Baste with pan juice every 15 minutes. In the last 15 minutes, using a pastry brush, coat the entire bird with your melted butter. Raise the temp to 400. Allow to cook until golden brown

This is the chicken Jane makes for Jake when they start their affair. It was the main course of his favorite meal.

The Five Worst Things To Say To Your Spouse

By Interfaith minister Stacey Y. Moore

What we say to the people we love is as important to them as what we do. Miguel Ruiz author of the highly acclaimed book, **The Four Agreements** teaches us that we should always be authentic with our words. We should say what we mean and mean what we say. Without knowing it most of us humans expect this to be the case, especially when we are dealing with a loved one.

We each believe or want to believe that the people talking to use are telling us the truth. With that in mind, here is a list of five things you should never say to your spouse and why.

1. **I am not attracted to you:** Telling your spouse that you are not attracted to them or that you find them unattractive is one of the most hurtful things you could possibly say. It begs the question, **"If you are not attracted to me… whom are you attracted to?"** Maybe you need to consider what you are calling attraction. Is it your physical response to their physical appearance? Is it based on your emotional attraction to their personality? Whatever it is that has changed in you; know that you are responsible for your own feelings, not your spouse. If you are not feeling attracted to them anymore perhaps you should consider getting therapy before you unload on your spouse.

2. **I am fine… when you are not**: Many times when we feel hurt or sad, we put on a stoic face and try to protect our loved ones from our pain. What we don't know is that they already feel it, and they may think that because we are not sharing the source of it, it must be them. If they are not the source, let them know. On the other hand, if they are the source you have to let them know that as well. When wounds (emotional ones especially) remain unhealed they tend to fester and grow bigger and more dangerous. Ask yourself, "why you feel bad", five times to get to the real source of your pain.

   For example:
   Why do I feel like crying? Because she/he hurt me. Why do I feel like she/he hurt me? Because of what she/he said. Why does what she/he said bother me? Because it was disrespectful. Why do I feel like he/she disrespected me? Because I don't like when people say ___. I find it disrespectful.

   This kind of internal dialog may help you to get to the core of the issue which may or may not be the fault of your partner, but may be in fact a personal issue that you have that you need to share with your partner.

3. **You don't _____ fill in the blank**: You don't love me, you don't care about me, you don't help me or even you don't deserve me, carries a lot of

weight. Often the word "don't" means, "never" to the person listening, and if there was ever a moment that you felt loved or cared for, then "don't" is not the correct term. Also, to say don't may be interpreted as, you did not appreciate it when they did (love you, care for you, or help you) and if you didn't appreciate it then, why should they do it again now. Don't make your spouse guess. Simply ask for the help or romantic gesture that you want. When you are missing a certain treatment or level of support, be specific in your request.

4. **You are just like your mother or father:** Unless your spouse's mother or father was granted sainthood by the Vatican, more than likely they don't want you comparing them to their parents. Most couples confide deeply in one another about their parent issues. To use a parent as a weapon in an argument is a double edged sword that will ultimately hurt both the wielder and the victim. In most families, the family members can talk about the other member's, but outsiders are not allowed to. To say that your spouse is just like their parent when you are obviously upset with their behavior is saying that you are also not happy with their parent's behavior, and strictly speaking, that is not your place.

5. **I really don't care:** This is a cop out and everyone knows it. If you really don't care, you should ask yourself, "Why don't I?" Obviously I am not talking about mundane things like McDonalds versus Taco Bell. I am talking about the big stuff like, I am gonna go out with the fellas/girls or my mother wants to stay here for a month or even, I want to buy a hot rod or an expensive purse. These types of proclamations/questions deserve a more heartfelt response because, I really don't care is basically code for, I don't give a F__k! By being unwilling to sort out your true feelings with your spouse, you are giving your spouse carte blanche on an issue that your relationship may not be able to afford.

Your turn - What are some things you know you should never say to your spouse?

_____

_____

_____

_____

_____

_____

_____

"If conversation was the lyrics, laughter was the music, making time spent together a melody that could be replayed over and over without getting stale."

— *Nicholas Sparks*

The Devil Wears Prada (2006)

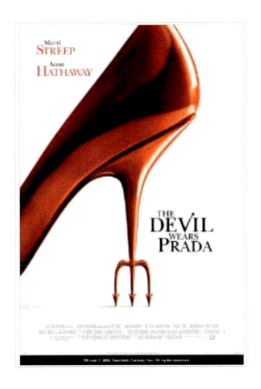

Writers: Aline Brosh McKenna (screenplay), Lauren Weisberger (novel), and Director: David Frankel , Starring Anne Hathaway, Meryl Streep, Adrian Grenier, Emily Blunt, Stanley Tucci, Simon Baker, Tracie Thoms.

Synopsis:
Andy and Nate are young, smart, broke, and in love. Both are dedicated to working their way into the careers of their dreams until Andy lands the job of a lifetime, but not of her dreams. Andy learns the hard way that decisions are hard to make when you are being unwittingly seduced by glamour.

The Devil Wears Prada~ Parmesan French Fries

CAST & CREW: Mise en place

3 large russet potatoes cut into medium fries
Vegetable oil for frying
Kosher salt
Fresh ground black pepper
Parmesan cheese

SCRIPT:

Begin by slicing potatoes and dropping the sliced fries into a large bowl of water to wash off any excess starch.

Heat a large pot of water and bring to a boil. Add enough salt so it tastes like the sea. Blanch potatoes in the boiling water and cook until tender -- about 4 minutes. Remove from water and strain then lay out in a flat layer and place in the freezer to cool and firm up.

Heat a Dutch oven or large fry pan filled 2/3rd of the way up with oil to 350-360 degrees. Fry the fries in small batches for 2-3 minutes until crispy on the outside and golden brown.

When golden brown, remove with a wire mesh strainer and place on a paper towel lined plate. Season with salt and pepper to taste. Garnish with Parmesan cheese

Andy and Nate eat out a lot but they really don't eat much. These fries were the meal Andy had at the restaurant where Nate works.

The Devil Wears Prada ~ Jarlsburg Grilled Cheese

CAST & CREW: Mise en place

4 slices sourdough bread
Two slices gruyere cheese
Butter

SCRIPT:

Butter each piece of bread on both sides.

Place a slice of cheese between two pieces of the bread to create a sandwich.

Warm a stove top grill over medium heat and place the sandwiches on the grill. Use a spatula to flatten the sandwiches in to the grill. Flip over and do it again.

Remove the sandwiches from the grill and serve.

Nate makes this high-end grilled cheese for Andy one evening in their apartment. They enjoy it with red wine.

Guess Who (2005)

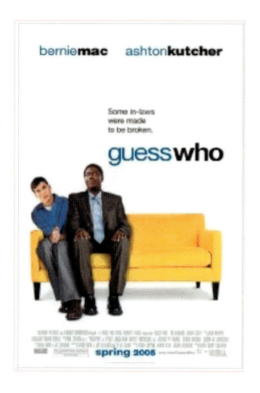

Director: Kevin Rodney Sullivan, Writers: William Rose (motion picture "Guess Who's Coming to Dinner"), Jay Scherick (screenplay) and Peter Tolan , (screenplay), David Ronn (story), Starring Bernie Mac, Zoe Saldana and Ashton Kutcher .

Synopsis:
When Theresa, brings her fiancé Simon home to meet her father Percy, she finds out that her father and her fiancé have a lot of growing up to do. This young interracial couple has to overcome racial tensions at home before they are ready to face the world as a family.

Guess Who – Pan Seared Chicken Fajitas

CAST & CREW: Mise en place
 2 lbs. Chicken breast strips,

Marinade:
1 lime, zest and juice
2 garlic cloves, finely sliced
3 tablespoon/s. roughly chopped fresh cilantro leaves
2 teaspoons ground cumin
1 teaspoon smoked paprika

1 teaspoon dark brown sugar
Kosher salt and freshly ground black pepper
1/4 cup olive oil

Vegetables:
1 White onion, sliced thick
1 red pepper, sliced into strips
1 green pepper, sliced into strips
Kosher salt and freshly ground black pepper
Extra-virgin olive oil
1 handful of fresh cilantro

SCRIPT:
In a mixing bowl combine marinade ingredients. Pour into a flat dish and add chicken. Massage ingredients into the chicken then cover with plastic wrap and set in the refrigerator to marinate for at least 45-60 minutes.

Next, marinade the vegetables: Toss all vegetables in to a mixing bowl. Coat with the oil and season with salt and pepper and set aside.

Heat a stainless steel pan over medium-high heat, and drizzle with olive oil. Remove chicken from marinade and sear for 6 or 7 minutes. Once browned, raise the heat to high and toss in the sliced vegetables and season with salt and pepper and stir quickly.

To serve, garnish with cilantro.

When the ladies are fed up with the men's lying and fighting, they take to the sanctity of a girl's night. The fajitas are interpretive.

Guess Who – Fresh Lemonade

CAST & CREW: Mise en place

1 cup freshly squeezed Meyers lemon juice (5 to 6 lemons)
1/2 to 3/4 cup superfine sugar, to taste
Fresh mint sprigs
4 cups water

SCRIPT:
Mix the lemon juice and sugar in a pitcher to create a simple syrup.

Next add the water and stir well. Taste for sweetness.

Add ice cubes and mint sprigs. Taste again and add more sugar if needed.

Serve over ice. Garnish with additional mint sprigs and lemon slices.

 This refreshing drink was seen throughout the movie.

Meet the Fockers (2004)

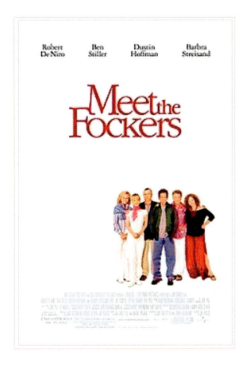

Writers: Greg Glienna (characters), Mary Ruth Clarke (characters), Directed by Jay Roach. With Ben Stiller, Robert De Niro, Blythe Danner, Teri Polo and Barbara Streisand.

Synopsis:
Greg and Pam are planning to get married but Pam's dad is a high strung professional buttinsky who has no boundaries when it comes to his family. Trying to keep Pam's high strung father from ruining their weekend is going to take some work.

Meet the Fockers ~ Fresh Vegetable Frittata

CAST & CREW: Mise en place

4 extra-large fresh eggs
Kosher salt and freshly ground black pepper
2 tablespoon(s) unsalted butter
1/2 cup heavy cream
1 clove of garlic, grated
1 cup grated smoked gouda cheese
1/2 small onion, diced
1 zucchini, sliced on the bias
1/2 cup green peas, blanched
2 small red potatoes diced
A handful of cherry or grape tomatoes
A few sprigs of (chives, chervil, and parsley), for garnish

SCRIPT:

Preheat oven to 450 degrees F.

In a large bowl, whisk together eggs and cream. Season with salt and pepper and set aside.

In an oven safe skillet add a little oil and sauté the zucchini, potatoes and onions until potatoes are tender. Add the peas, tomatoes and garlic then reduce the heat to low.

Pour the egg mixture into the pan coating the vegetables. With a wooden spoon move the eggs around. Continue to do this over low heat for a few minutes. Next, top the frittata with plenty of grated smoked Gouda.

Place the pan in the oven and bake until the frittata has puffed up and is slightly golden around the edges. Garnish with some fresh torn herbs, a drizzle of olive oil and some cracked black pepper.

 This dish can be seen in the family breakfast scene.

Meet the Fockers ~ Grand Tom Collins

CAST & CREW: Mise en place

4oz gin
2 oz lemon juice
2 teaspoon(s) superfine sugar
2 oz. Grand Marnier
6 oz. club soda
2 maraschino cherries
2 slice orange slices

SCRIPT:

Fill a cocktail shaker halfway with ice cubes; add the gin, lemon juice, Grand Marnier and sugar.

With the lid on, give it a good shake.

Strain into a glasses over ice cubes. Add the club soda. Stir and garnish with the cherry and the orange slice.

This drink was prepared by the Fockers, Rozalin and Bernie during the first meeting of the Fockers and the Byrnes family.

10 GREAT WAYS TO KEEP YOUR RELATIONSHIP FUN!

BY INTERFAITH MINISTER STACEY Y. MOORE

Author and educator, Bell Hooks explained that there are two reasons for discontentment in a relationship: 1) A person fails at making another person happy, or 2) A person succeeds at making the other person unhappy. Keeping the spark ablaze in a relationship deals directly with number one.

How fun are you to live with?
We each must make it our business to keep our relationships fun which in turn should keep our partners happy. With this in mind I have to pose a question that I lifted from Dr. Phil, **"How fun are you to live with?"** I can tell you now that nothing sucks the life from a relationship better or faster than living with a sad, dull, miserable or just plain ole un-fun individual. If that blasé person is you… it's time to liven up the game. The best part of it is, if you are making life fun for your partner, you will also be making life fun for yourself.

In my mind the best way to keep the flame alive is to, keep-the-fun-a-comin. Here is a sample list of ways to up the fun in your relationship. This list is not age specific, no matter how old you are, go for it. Also, use this as a tool to create your own fun list.

1. **Play hide and seek at night… nude**! In your own home of course.

2. **Play strip poker, strip tonk or strip go-fish;** whatever your game is, play for your clothes.

3. **Take a nature walk together**, listen to the birds, and enjoy being outdoors.

4. **Have a pic-nic** in the living room on a rainy day or a sunny day.

5. **Take a real shower together**, suds each other's backs, use sea salts or full body mud masks.

6. **Turn the TV off and listen to music** together at dinner time. Better yet, dance.

7. **Sing to each other**; sing to strangers together - Go Karaoke- ing.

8. Discover new restaurants together. **Get out of your ten mile radius**.

9. Touch each other in sensitive places; in other words, **tickle each other**.

10. **Build something cool together**. It can be as simple as a meal.

Your turn - Create your own list of fun To Dos:

_____
_____
_____
_____
_____
_____
_____

"Marriage, ultimately, is the practice of becoming passionate friends."
-Harville Hendrix

"I would love you all the day, every night we would kiss and play, if with me you'd fondly stray, over the hills and far away."

— John Gray

Jumping the Broom (2011)

Director Salim Akil, Writers Elizabeth Hunter (screenplay), Arlene Gibbs (screenplay), Stars: Paula Patton, Laz Alonso, Angela Bassett, Loretta Devine, Meagan Good and Tasha Smith, Featuring Rev. T.D Jakes.

Synopsis:

Cultures collide when a young couple from very different sides of the tracks fall in love and plan an upper crust wedding. Tempers soar and attitudes are revealed during the weekend long festivities. Is love enough when you don't have familial foundations in common? This lovely you couple will find out.

Jumping the Broom-Baked Champagne Oysters on the Half

CAST & CREW: Mise en place

1 dozen fresh oysters, shucked on the half shell

Sauce:
1 small shallot, very finely chopped
¼ red pepper chopped fine
3 tablespoons of butter
1/4 cup champagne or dry sparkling wine
2 lemons
Kosher salt and freshly ground black pepper
2 teaspoons of finely chopped tarragon

SCRIPT:

Preheat broiler or grill. Place oysters on a bed of crumpled foil (to hold them in place) on a roasting tray. Place under the broiler for 60-90 seconds or on the grill (lid closed) until oysters are warm and slightly bubbly.

Champagne Sauce: over medium- low heat warm a small saucepan. Add the butter and shallots and peppers. Simmer slowly but do not brown. Add the champagne and let it simmer until slightly reduced. Season with salt and pepper.

Remove oysters from oven and top each oyster with a teaspoon of the champagne sauce while they are still warm. Garnish with a little tarragon and lemon wedges.

The sexy chef for the event, shares a variation of this amorous appetizer with the maid of honor.

Jumping the Broom - Chilled Poached Shrimp

CAST & CREW: Mise en place

1 lb. of large shrimp, unpeeled
Lemon slices and parsley for garnish

Court Bouillon:
1 bottle (17 fl. oz.) of lager beer
1 bay leaf
2 sprigs of fresh thyme
1 cup of Old Bay seasoning
4 cloves of garlic
1 orange, cut in half
1 whole onion
Salt and pepper to taste

SCRIPT:

Begin by preparing the court bouillon. In a large stock pot, fill two-quarters of the way up with water and add court bouillon ingredients. Stir well and bring up to a rolling boil.

Once the court bouillon is boiling add the shrimp, then shut off the heat and allow the shrimp to cook in the heat of the liquid. Cover and let it sit for 5-7 minutes.

Use a wire mesh strainer to get the shrimp out of the pot. Chill in the refrigerator for one hour.

Serve on cracked ice in individual cocktail glasses. Garnish with fresh lemon wedges.

 The bride's family served chilled shrimp at the pre-rehearsal meet and greet.

Jumping the Broom-Mimosas

CAST & CREW: Mise en place

1 750 ml bottle chilled dry sparkling wine
2 cups (750 ml) chilled orange juice (freshly squeezed is best)
1/2 cup (118 ml) Grand Marnier or triple sec (optional)

SCRIPT:

Fill 8 champagne flutes 1/2 full with chilled sparkling wine. Top with orange juice.

Top mimosa with 1 tablespoon of Grand Marnier or triple sec.

This is the sassy but classy dish ordered by Tom's girlfriend right before she breaks up with him at Amanda's restaurant.

Guided Movie Discussion
Based on the University of Rochester study

1. What was the nature of the main relationship in the movie?

2. Discuss the problems faced by the couple. Do you face them in your relationship?

3. How well did the couple relate to one another? Were they acceptant of each other's differences?

    a. In what ways is your relationship similar to or different from theirs?

4. Did the couple share a friendship with each other? How did they show consideration for each other? How did they communicate with each other? Did they have fun with each other, if so, by doing what? Did they take care of each other?

    a. In what ways is your relationship similar to or different from theirs?

5. How did the couple handle disagreements? Did they work together to gain understanding of each other's discontent? Did they show respect for each other's opinions or positions?

    a. In what ways is your relationship similar to or different from theirs?

6. How heated were the couple's arguments? Did they fight fair or did they resort to name calling and yelling? Did they have a plan in place for how to handle disagreements?

    a. In what ways is your relationship similar to or different from theirs?

7. When discussing a problem or issue, did the couple bring up the issue in a loving and constructive way or did they focus on the negative feelings they had rather than the issue?

    a. In what ways is your relationship similar to or different from theirs?

8. How well did the couple accept responsibility when one was wrong or insensitive to the other's feelings?

    a. In what ways is your relationship similar to or different from theirs?

9. Did the couple share expectations or were their expectations different from each other's? Did each person understand the other person's expectations?

    a. In what ways is your relationship similar to or different from theirs?

10. What events in the movie have made you think differently about your marriage?

11. What else did you learn from this movie?

Quick Cooking Techniques

Croutons

CAST & CREW:

5 slices of French bread
1/4 cup olive oil
1 Clove fresh garlic peeled
Dry thyme
Salt to taste

SCRIPT:

Preheat oven to 350 degrees F (175 degrees C).

Brush bread on both sides with olive oil. Cut bread slices up into small cubes. Sprinkle with salt and thyme

Use the flat of your knife to crush the garlic clove on your cutting board. Take the garlic and rub it all over a cooking sheet.

Arrange cubes on the cookie sheet.

Bake for 15 minutes or until browned. Let cool. Serve in soups or salads

Egg Poaching:

Crack eggs one at a time and place each in a separate cup or small bowl and set aside.

Heat water for poaching: Put 2-inches of water in a large pan add, and vinegar and bring to a gentle simmer over medium heat. The water should not be moving much.

Using a spoon swirl the hot water in a circular motion to create a whirlpool effect. Gently slide one egg in at a time.

Cook until the whites are set and opaque, about 3 minutes. Remove the eggs from the water with a slotted spoon and trim the edges to tidy them up if necessary.

Hollandaise Sauce:

CAST & CREW:

3 egg yolks
½ lemon, juiced
1 teaspoon cold water
1 teaspoon salt
1 teaspoon ground black pepper
½ cup butter

SCRIPT:

In a small bowl, whisk together egg yolks, lemon juice, cold water, salt and pepper.

Melt butter in a saucepan over low heat.

Gradually whisk yolk mixture into butter. Continue whisking over low heat for 8 minutes or until sauce is thickened. Serve immediately.

Mayonnaise:

CAST & CREW:

1 large egg yolk
1 ½ teaspoons fresh lemon juice
1 teaspoon white wine vinegar
¼ teaspoon Dijon mustard
½ teaspoon salt plus more to taste
¾ cup canola oil, divided

SCRIPT:

In a medium bowl whisk together egg yolk, lemon juice, vinegar, mustard, and ½ teaspoon salt until completely blended and bright yellow.

Whisking constantly, add ¼ cup oil to egg mixture very slowly, only a few drops at a time. Gradually add remaining ½ cup oil in very slow thin stream, whisking constantly, until mayonnaise is thick, about 8 minutes (mayonnaise will be lighter in color). Cover and chill.

Mire Poix: Classic

CAST & CREW:

Carrots, Onion and Celery

SCRIPT:

Use two parts onion to one part carrot and one part celery -- clean, trim and cut into any evenly-sized shape.

Place ingredients in a pan with 2 tablespoons of butter, or olive oil and cook over medium heat until translucent.

Mise en place:

A French phrase which means "putting in place", or set up. in professional kitchens it is used to refer to organizing and arranging the ingredients (e.g., cuts of meat, relishes, sauces, par-cooked items, spices, freshly chopped vegetables, and other components) that a cook will require for the menu items that are expected to be prepared during a shift.

Muscle and Clam (Mollusks) Cleaning:

Before cooking mussels or clams, be sure to scrub the shells in cold water with a stiff brush to remove barnacles and sand. Soaking them in cold water mixed with a few handfuls of cornmeal for 30 to 60 minutes will reduce the amount of interior sand.

Debearding Mollusks:

Protruding between the shells is a small bristle or beard, which the mollusk uses to attach itself to rocks and surfaces. Before cooking, remove the beard by tightly grasping the hairs near their base with your fingers or pliers and giving a hard pull. The beard should come right out.

Mushroom Cleaning:

Because they are sponge like and absorb water easily, mushrooms won't brown very well when cooked if they are soaked in water. Instead, use a damp paper towel or a soft mushroom brush to wipe each mushroom, one at a time, to remove any dirt. You can also lightly rinse the mushrooms with cool water and pat dry with paper towels.

Peeling Tomatoes:

Boil a pot of water over high heat.

Take each tomatoes and put a ¼ inch cross cut on the top and bottom, only cutting the skin and not deep into the flesh. Set them in a heat resistant bowl such as glass or stainless-steel.

Pour the boiling water over the top of the tomatoes covering them entirely. Allow to sit for 2 minutes.

Pour off the hot water and fill the bowl with cold water. The skin will blister.

Peel the skin of the tomatoes gently with the tip of a sharp knife.

Stock: Chicken or Beef Stock:

CAST & CREW:

2 to 3 lbs. leftover bones and skin from a cooked or raw chicken carcass or beef bones
2 Celery stalks – cut in to large pieces
1 whole onions –peeled and halved
2 carrots – Cut into large pieces
3 sprigs of Parsley
3 sprigs of Thyme
2 garlic cloves - peeled
2 bay leaves
Salt and Pepper
Olive oil

SCRIPT:

In a large pot over medium-high heat, warm a tablespoon of olive oil. Add vegetables and herbs. Sauté for about 3 minutes. Add salt and pepper. Put the Beef or chicken bones into the pot and cover with cold water.

Bring to a boil and immediately reduce heat to bring the stock to barely a simmer. Simmer uncovered at least 4 hours; occasionally skim off the foam that comes to the surface with a large spoon.

Remove the bones with a slotted spoon and strain the stock. It can be refrigerated for up to 5 days.

Note: For a brown stock, roast the bones first and don't peel the onion.

"Coming together is a beginning; keeping together is progress; working together is success."

-Henry Ford

Research Credits

Martell, Ashley , Cooking With Your Spouse Strengthens Relationships, October 29, 2014
http://foodal.com/knowledge/how-to/cooking-spouse-stengthens-relationships/ (pg. 7)

Foley, Todd, Cook your way toward a healthier marriage, 2012
http://www.focusonthefamily.ca/marriage/first-five-years/cook-your-way-toward-a-healthier-marriage (pg. 7)

Hagen, Susan, Divorce Rate Cut in Half for Couples Who Discussed Relationship Movies: A study conducted by Ronald D. Rogge, PhD Associate Professor of Psychology et al, at the University of Rochester' January 31, 2014. (pg. 7 and pg. 71)
http://www.rochester.edu/news/divorce-rate-cut-in-half-for-couples-who-discussed-relationship-movies/.

Tara Parker-Pope, New York Times, **Movie Date Night Can Double as Therapy**,
http://well.blogs.nytimes.com/2014/02/10/movie-date-night-can-double-as-therapy/?_r=0, February 10, 2014. (pg. 7)

Sharon Jayson, USA TODAY, **Party of four? A double date can rev up your romance**,
http://www.usatoday.com/story/news/nation/2014/02/10/passion-research-double-date/5289181/,
February 10, 2014. (pg. 7)

Cooking Methods Research

Top Chef University at http://www.topchefuniversity.com/   2014
(pg. 72-75)

Movie Credits (in the order they appear)

Date Night
Production company Dune Entertainment, 21 Laps and Media Magik Entertainment
Distributed by 20th Century Fox, Release date April 6, 2010 - Wikipedia. (pg. 7)

The Five Year Engagement
Production companies Apatow Productions and Relativity Media
Distributed by Universal Pictures, Release date April 27, 2012 – Wikipedia. (pg. 12)

Julie and Julia
Production company Columbia Pictures. Distributed by Sony Pictures Releasing
Release date August 7, 2009 – Wikipedia. (pg.15)

Soul Food
Fox 2000 Pictures, Edmonds Entertainment Group (EEG), 1997 (pg. 21)

Sex and the City
Production Companies New Line Cinema (presents),Home Box Office (HBO) (in association with) Darren Star Productions (as A Darren Star Production). Distribution companies New Line Cinema (2008) (USA) (theatrical) , Warner Home Video (2008) (USA) (DVD) – imdb. (pg. 26)

Think Like A Man
Production Companies Screen Gems (presents) and Rainforest Films. Distributed by, Screen Gems (2012) (USA) (theatrical), Sony Pictures Releasing.- imdb. (pg.32)

This Is 40
Production Companies Apatow Productions (as Apatow) and Forty Productions(uncredited) Distributed by, Universal Pictures (2012) – imdb. (pg.37)

It's Complicated
Universal Pictures, Relativity Media, Waverly Films, 2009 (pg. 42)

The Devil Wears Prada
Production Companies Fox 2000 Pictures (presents), (A Wendy Finerman Production), Dune Entertainment (made in association with) (as Dune Entertainment LLC), Major Studio Partners (made in association with), Twentieth Century Fox Film Corporation (uncredited) and Peninsula Films (executive production) (uncredited). Distributed by, Twentieth Century Fox Film Corporation (2006) (World-wide) (all media) (as 20th Century Fox) – imdb. (pg.48)

Guess Who
Production companies Columbia Pictures Corporation (presents) (as Columbia Pictures), Regency Enterprises (presents), 3 Art Entertainment (as 3 Arts), Tall Trees Productions (as Tall Trees), Katalyst Filmsand Epsilon Motion Pictures (uncredited). Distribution by Columbia Pictures (2005) (USA) (theatrical) (a Sony Pictures Entertainment company) –imdb. (pg.51)

Meet the Fockers
Production Companies Universal Pictures (presents), DreamWorks SKG (presents), Tribeca Productions and Everyman Pictures. Distribution by, Universal Pictures (2004) (USA) (all media) – imdb. (pg. 54)

Jumping the Broom
Production Companies TriStar Pictures (presents), Stage 6 Films (in association with), Our Stories Films, Sony Pictures Worldwide Acquisitions (SPWA) and TDJ Enterprises / New Dimensions Entertainment. Distribution by, TriStar Pictures (2011) (USA) (theatrical) – imdb. (pg. 59)

About the Author

Stacey "The Movie Foodie" Moore,
Wedding officiant and Marriage and Relationship Educator

Stacey Y. Moore knows the recipe for creating great relationships. Being a popular wedding officiant for 8 years, delivering heartfelt, upbeat, non-denominational wedding ceremonies in the Dallas, Fort Worth Metroplex, has taught Stacey a thing or two about love and marriage. Her mission is to help couples relationships grow stronger and last longer. Armed with a degree in Communication Studies with a minor in Psychology and life… she openly shares everything she knows about building better relationships with the couples she works with. Couples can count on Stacey to be strait forward in her conversations about love and marriage. She is a talented natural cook with a penchant for recreating movie food, which makes her a trustworthy, fun and entertaining source for relationship, recipes and cooking advice.

Need a speaker for your next event?
Stacey is an engaging and charming public speaker, and is available for special events globally. For information on booking Stacey to speak and or present movie food cooking techniques at you next event, go to:
http://www.felliniskitchen.com/about-us.html or
www.weddingministernow.com

Made in the USA
Monee, IL
29 November 2020